CULTURE ENCYCLOPEDIA

HISTORY OF CULTURE

CULTURE ENCYCLOPEDIA
HISTORY OF
CULTURE

Fiona MacDonald

Mason Crest

Mason Crest Publishers Inc.
370 Reed Road
Broomall, PA 19008
(866) MCP-BOOK (toll free)
www.masoncrest.com
This edition first published in 2003

First published by Miles Kelly Publishing,
Bardfield Centre, Great Bardfield, Essex, CM7 4SL, U.K.
Copyright © Miles Kelly Publishing 2002, 2003

2 4 6 8 10 9 7 5 3 1

Library of Congress Cataloging-in-Publication Data on file
at the Library of Congress

ISBN 1-59084-477-7

Author
Fiona MacDonald

Designed and Edited by
Starry Dog Books

Project Editor
Belinda Gallagher

Assistant Editors
Mark Darling, Nicola Jessop, Isla Macuish

Artwork Commissioning
Lesley Cartlidge

Indexer
Jane Parker

Picture Research
Ruth Boardman, Liberty Newton

Color Reproduction
DPI Colour, Saffron Walden, Essex, UK

Printed in China

Contents

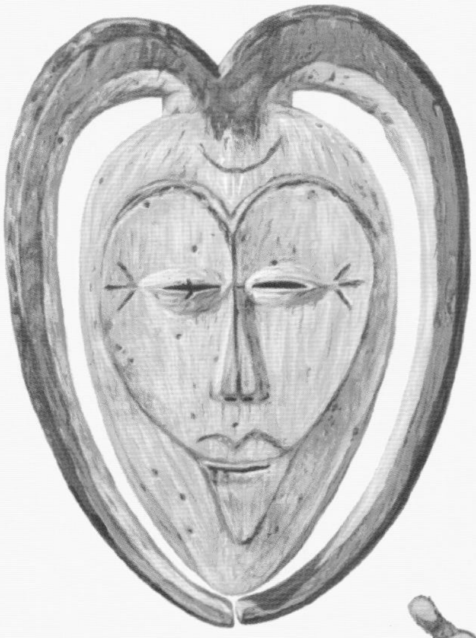

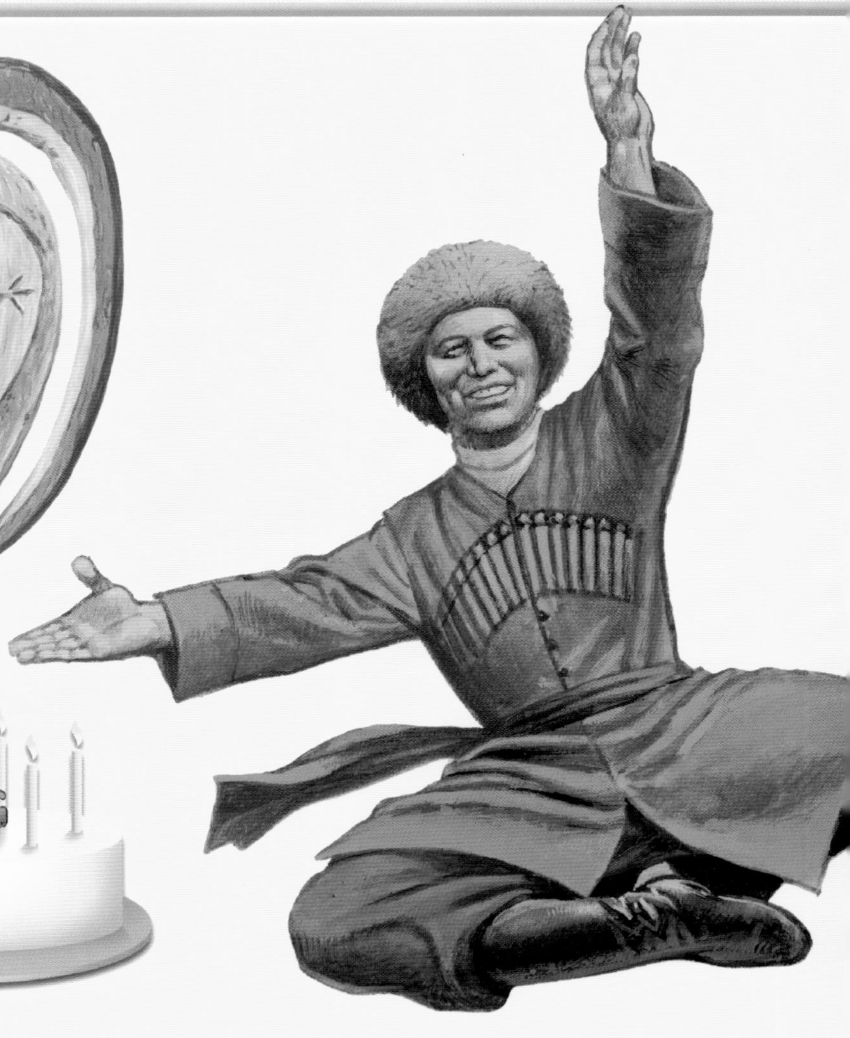

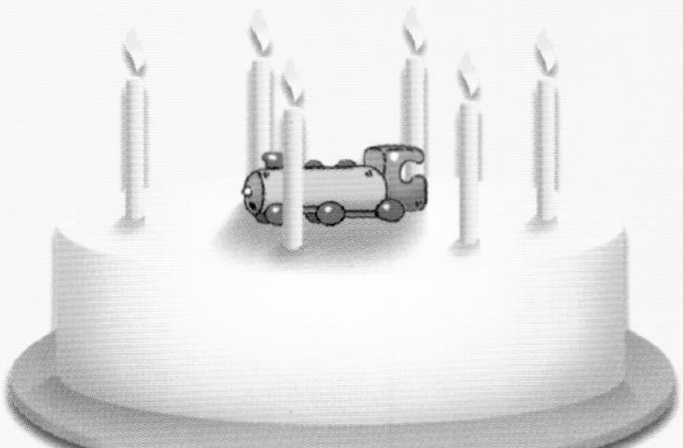

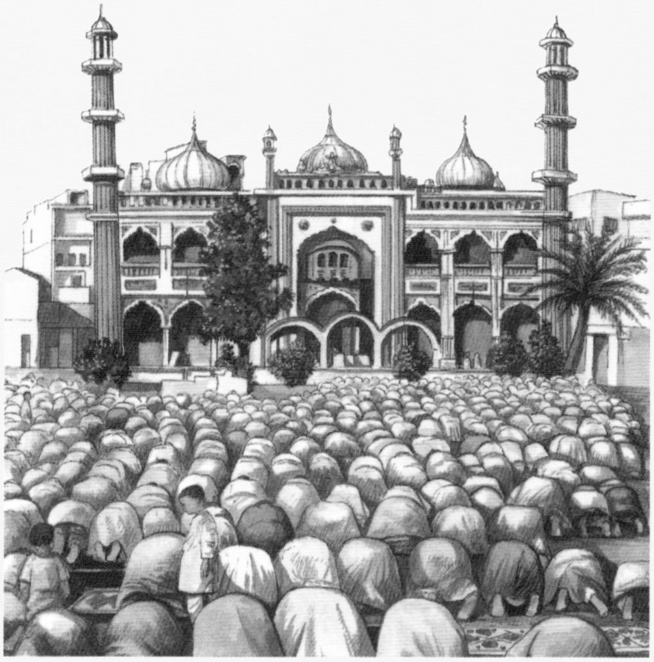

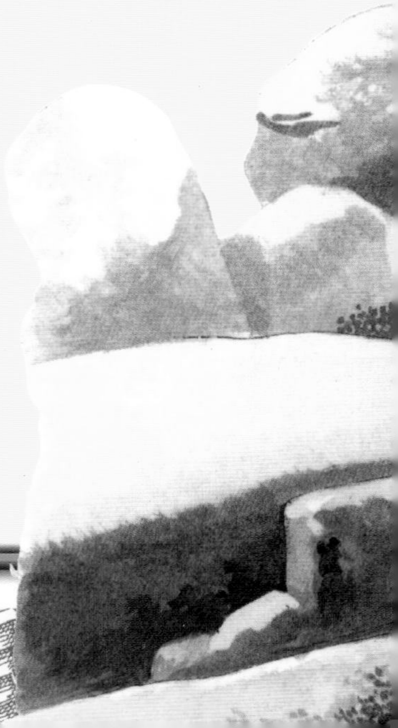

History of Culture

THE word "culture" is often used to describe art forms that are enjoyed by only a few people—such as opera or ballet. But "culture" can mean much more than that. It can describe someone's upbringing and education, religious faith, community's traditions, and nation's language, literature, and art. It can also describe how a person lives, his or her political ideas, and how he or she identifies themselves. Usually, "culture" refers to all these things together, and is used to describe a unique civilization of a particular time or people.

What does culture do?

WITHIN each society or civilization, culture has many separate functions. Books, films, plays, and music can simply amuse and entertain, or they can be challenging and thought-provoking. They can reinforce traditional values, or inspire people with unsettling new ideas. Practicing ancient forms of culture—from craftwork to folk dancing—can be a way of preserving a treasured heritage, or maintaining a threatened way of life. During the 20th century, mass culture became a valuable commodity, sold by global corporations to consumers in many lands.

◤ ANCIENT CULTURE

The Roma people—sometimes known as "Gypsies"—have preserved their ancient nomadic way of life for hundreds of years, along with their own language, customs, crafts, and musical traditions. Originally from northern India, Roma now live in many parts of Europe and northern Africa.

◤ SEGREGATION

Ideas about culture often play an important part in politics. In South Africa, from the 1950s to the 1990s, the white rulers forced black and white people to be kept apart, or segregated, claiming that white culture was "better" than the local African civilization.

◣ MASS MEDIA

During the 20th century, mass media—films, TV, and magazines—were able to reach a worldwide audience. Children were no longer entertained just by local or regional stories. Although films made in the West, such as *The Lion King,* are hugely popular, they can also weaken local cultures.

▷ FOLK FESTIVAL

Around 1800, the Industrial Revolution changed the way people lived. Many skills and crafts died out. But people like these Breton folk dancers from France keep alive their culture by celebrating it in folk festivals.

◢ TRADITIONAL LIFESTYLE

For many peoples, following their traditional lifestyle is a way of keeping their culture alive. In northwest Canada, for example, some Inuit men still hunt seals for their skins, meat, and blubber, waiting for the seals to surface at ice holes.

◩ HIGH CULTURE

Opera stars such as Russian singer Galina Vishnevskaya, spend many years training to reach international standards. Only the best succeed. Opera music is often described as "high culture"—because it can be difficult to understand, and is not popular with everyone.

NATIONAL PRIDE

On July 4, Americans celebrate their independence from British rule by having a national Independence Day holiday. The national flag—"The Star-Spangled Banner"— is flown proudly everywhere.

Belonging

FOR most people, a sense of belonging is very important. People like—and need—to feel that they are not alone. Most people feel love or loyalty towards a small group, such as their family. Some are loyal to large organizations, such as the company they work for, or their school. Many people also feel deeply attached to the place where they live, or to the country where they were born. Belonging to a political party can be important, too. And increasingly, young people show loyalty to designer logos or well-known brands. All these feelings of belonging help define, or shape, the culture of individuals and whole communities.

◢ THE "BIG M"
Many international corporations, such as McDonald's, use a logo on all their buildings and products. The logo attracts customers anywhere in the world. When people see it, they feel safe, because they know exactly what products the company sells.

◣ HOLY SIGN
The cross on the roof of this simple white building in Greece tells passers-by that it is a Christian church. For Christians, the cross is a holy sign. It reminds them of the wooden frame on which Jesus Christ was executed in about AD 30. People from other faiths also use holy signs. Muslims use a crescent moon to symbolize Islam, and Jewish people use a six-pointed Star of David.

◢ RITUAL OF SHARING
In many Christian churches, the most important religious ceremony involves sharing holy bread and wine. Worshipers take part in this ritual—called the Mass, Holy Communion, or Eucharist—to feel closer to God and to their fellow Christians. The ritual recalls Christ's Last Supper with his disciples.

◄ TEAM COLORS

Members of national or local sports teams all wear the same style of clothing, in the same colors. This helps them identify other team members on the field, when play is fast and furious. Wearing identical clothes also helps build team spirit—the players are united not just in appearance, but also in their loyalty to each other and their desire to beat the opposition.

▷ WEDDING RINGS

Married couples in many countries wear wedding rings to show their lifelong commitment to one another. The custom of wearing a wedding ring on the fourth finger of the left hand originated in Europe, probably over 2,000 years ago. People believed that a vein from this finger led to the heart.

FLAGS

Flags originated as banners, carried to help soldiers follow their leaders into battle. Now they are important national symbols, carried in processions at international events and flown on public holidays. These are the flags of Asia.

☑ IN UNIFORM

Dressed in uniform, these U.S. guards of honor are lined up on parade for inspection. For all armed forces and public services, such as the police, uniforms are a sign of belonging. Officers demand very high standards of neatness as a way of encouraging self-respect and discipline.

Words and music

THROUGHOUT history, different cultures have expressed their values, beliefs, and ideas in poems, songs, and stories. Through the spoken or written word, a culture's beliefs were communicated to the wider world. In the past, different traditions in words and music identified groups within each society—and sometimes caused quarrels between peoples or nations. Today, people can enjoy an amazing variety of styles— some modern, others from long ago, or from far-distant countries with very different cultures.

◪ CHURCH CHRONICLE
Some of the earliest history writers were medieval monks. They wrote brief comments about important events in the margins of official church calendars. Their comments were collected together as "chronicles."

◪ MESSENGER
The Incas of South America (c. AD 1100 to 1530) ruled a huge empire. Unable to read or write, they used relay runners, called *chasquis*, to memorize and carry messages across the Andes Mountains.

◪ FIRESIDE TALE
During the 19th century, families gathered round the fire to listen to stories told by grandparents. Passing on stories and anecdotes from one generation to the next was a way of keeping a culture's beliefs and values alive. Many stories contained a message that taught young people how to behave.

MINSTREL

Medieval minstrels played to entertain lords and ladies in their castles. They often composed their own songs and poems, praising brave heroes or beautiful women. Minstrels were especially famous for writing songs about romantic love. For hundreds of years after their music was forgotten, their ideas remained popular in Europe.

NOBLE POETESS

In many civilizations, learning how to write poetry was part of every nobleman's education. A few noblewomen learned, too, including Sei Shonagon, who lived at the royal court in Japan (c. 966 to 1017).

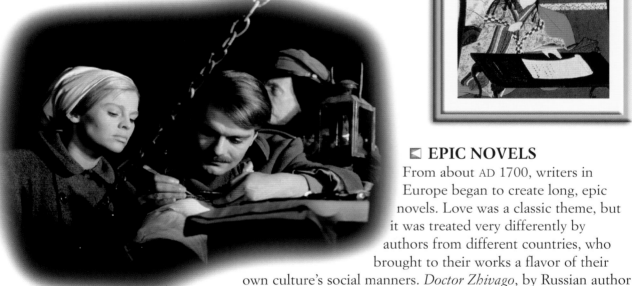

EPIC NOVELS

From about AD 1700, writers in Europe began to create long, epic novels. Love was a classic theme, but it was treated very differently by authors from different countries, who brought to their works a flavor of their own culture's social manners. *Doctor Zhivago*, by Russian author Boris Pasternak (1890–1960), combines passion with political drama.

GOOD VERSUS EVIL

All around the world, traditional stories describe battles between the forces of good and evil. Often, these tales have a religious or political meaning, and are hundreds of years old. During the 20th century, American movie makers used the theme of good versus evil to create some of their most successful stories. Westerns, gangster films, spy movies, and space adventures, such as *Star Wars*, all feature fights between characters representing good and evil.

Houses and homes

TODAY, just as in the past, people's houses are shaped by many different factors, such as their wealth, rank, and the size of their family. The design and construction of people's homes is also influenced by the climate, by local building techniques, and by what materials are available. The layout of a house is often closely linked to a culture's ideas about the right way to live. In countries where women are not expected to work outside the home. For example, some houses are built with separate female quarters, and craftworkers' homes may include a workshop.

◥ THATCHED ROOF

Many traditional building styles are hundreds of years old. This stone-walled, straw-thatched house in Peru is built to a design used by the Incas, who ruled the Andes over 500 years ago. Like Inca houses, it has a walled courtyard.

◹ ROCK HOUSE

Some of the earliest human houses, made over 50,000 years ago, were simple shelters built in the mouths of caves or under overhanging rocks. This house in Portugal is based on the same ancient idea. It uses a natural feature in the landscape to provide a person with rugged protection from the wind and rain.

◀ PAPER WALLS

In Japan, traditional houses were designed to withstand frequent earthquakes. Their walls were made of paper stretched over bamboo poles. If an earthquake was slight, the walls would tremble but stay up. If it was severe, they would collapse without killing the people inside.

✓ IRON AND GLASS

Tall "skyscraper" office and apartment buildings tower over Lake Chicago, Illinois. The world's first skyscraper, which was made using a strong metal frame, was designed in 1885. Now, skyscrapers dominate the skyline of most modern cities, and range from poor housing to stylish offices.

✓ LOG CABIN

In regions with plentiful timber, such as Canada, Russia, and northern Europe, many traditional homes are built of wood—a cheaper material than imported brick or stone.

MOVABLE HOME

Nomadic peoples, like the Mongols of Central Asia, live in homes that are easy to move. The Mongols take their "yurts"— domed tents made of thick felt—with them when they go in search of new grazing land for their flocks.

✓ STATELY HOME

Some of the world's most splendid houses were built for nobility and royalty, by the most skilled builders and craftworkers. This grand house with its elegant garden was designed for a noble family in Portugal, about 1670.

Food for all

FOOD plays an important part in the world's many different cultures. In some countries, such as Italy or India, it is immensely varied from one region to another. But universally, eating good food is enjoyed. In many cultures, sharing food with other people is considered a duty, and is a tradition that dates back thousands of years. As soon as early humans learned to grow crops, peasants spent their lives growing, cooking, and preserving food to feed their families. Today, many people are still employed in farming and fishing, as well as in food-processing factories and supermarkets. But although people in richer countries can eat foods from anywhere in the world at any time of year, many people in poorer regions continue to face starvation.

◤ EATING TOGETHER
Sharing a meal, as this Japanese-American family is doing, is one of the oldest pleasures known. It is a way for family members to come together at the end of a busy day to share their news and enjoy their favorite food. For Asian people, it is a cultural tradition to eat food using two chopsticks held in one hand.

◀ RICE GROWING
In east Asia, rice has been grown in flooded paddies for thousands of years. In the past, local communities depended on food crops grown in the nearby fields. But today, many of the food crops grown by people in poor countries are sent to feed the people of rich nations.

◰ SUPERMARKET
The first supermarkets opened in about the 1950s. For the first time, people could help themselves to prepackaged goods displayed on open shelves. Supermarkets claim to make shopping faster, easier, and more enjoyable. But some people today argue that they have too much control over the farmers who produce the food.

FOOD AID

Famines are often the result of natural disasters, or too much or too little rainfall. Emergency supplies from other countries are sent by truck to people in need.

◣ FOOD FOR FUN

In countries where the weather is dry and sunny for much of the year, outdoor cooking is very popular. Simple food, such as steaks or sausages, are grilled over charcoal on a "barbecue." The word means "frame of sticks," and originated in the Caribbean.

◤ FAST FOOD

Burger and fries are a favorite "fast food"—a meal that comes in a box and can be eaten at table or carried out. Prepared in huge quantities in factories, the food items are shipped for final cooking to "outlets" all over the world. The cooking and serving procedures are strictly controlled. Although fast food is extremely popular, food experts fear that eating too much of it is unhealthy.

◧ OFF TO MARKET

In Africa and many other parts of the developing world, women grow food for their families on small garden plots. They carry any surplus produce, like these bananas—which will rot if not eaten quickly—to local markets to sell. This may mean a long journey, for little pay.

Looking good

HOW can a person tell which culture someone else belongs to? Mostly, they can find clues in the person's clothes, hairstyle, and make-up—all of which tell us something about who the other person is. Clothes may reflect someone's religion, their ethnic origin, or even their political views. A uniform provides information about skills, training or rank. Traditional "costumes" are often woven by hand from natural fibers, and may be decorated with local patterns. Fashion items are often made from artificial fibers and are produced in great quantities in factories. They may display popular designer labels.

◪ NATIONAL DRESS
National costumes, like these from 19th-century Hungary, are a symbol of pride and are closely linked to the local culture. They reflect local weather, products (wool or silk), and ideas about decency.

◪ OLD AND YOUNG
Old people and young children prefer to dress in their own styles. The elderly often choose formal clothes that follow a tradition, while children like to wear the latest fashions. Teenagers enjoy wearing clothes that rebel against formal traditions and shock older generations.

▭ SPORTS OUTFITS
Sports clothes, like the tops and pants worn by these gymnasts, are highly specialized. The fabric needs to bend and stretch with the body, fit closely, and be light, comfortable, and hard-wearing. The earliest sports clothes were made of natural fibers such as wool and cotton. Today, high-tech artificial fibers are used.

◪ FINISHING TOUCHES

A person who wears a neat hairstyle, makeup, and jewelry is indicating to others that he or she cares about his or her appearance and wants to look good. These adornments can indicate if they are rich or poor, married or single. This African girl has taken great care plaiting her many tiny braids, while her large metal earrings are a sign of wealth.

◪ DRESSED FOR PRAYER

Many different faiths teach that men and women should be modestly dressed in public, and that they should wear special clothes when performing religious rituals as a sign of respect. These Muslim women, who are on holy pilgrimage, have covered their heads and shoulders with a simple white garment. Jewish men also cover their heads and shoulders while reading from holy scriptures.

PROTEST CLOTHES

During the 1920s, young women "flappers" cut their hair short, stopped wearing tight, uncomfortable corsets, and wore daringly short skirts as a way of demanding personal freedom and women's political rights.

◪ WESTERN STYLE

During the 20th century, many peoples all around the world stopped dressing in traditional costumes and began to wear Western-style clothes—as a way of showing that they had modern ideas. This Asian woman, for example, is wearing Western-style clothes while riding to work on her bicycle.

Life cycles

ALL around the world, people from different cultures have invented ceremonies to mark the important stages of a person's life. New babies are welcomed with naming rituals, or with ceremonies that enroll them in a particular religion. In many cultures, older children have to perform "initiation" rituals, which are a way of proclaiming that they have reached adulthood. Marriage is often marked by rejoicing, and by an exchange of property between families. In many traditional cultures, the elderly are treated with respect. Almost everywhere, dead people are laid to rest with funeral prayers, which often express hope in a new life after death.

◹ INITIATION MASK
In many parts of the world, the change from childhood to adulthood is marked by special rituals. Groups of young men and women are taken away from their families to spend weeks with respected elders, who teach them local traditions and encourage them to develop skills they will need in adult life. Some take part in singing and dancing and wear masks, like this one from Africa.

◹ ROYAL BIRTH
Most families share their pleasure at the birth of a new baby with their neighbors and friends. But rejoicing spreads to a wider public when the new baby is a royal prince or princess. This 16th-century painting from India shows people celebrating the birth of the Mongol prince, Timur, who later ruled Samarkand in Central Asia.

◸ GRAND MEMORIAL
Few people want to be forgotten after they are dead. Some are happy to be remembered by the people who have loved them. But others plan splendid monuments, like these temple-tombs in Madhya Pradesh, India. Powerful leaders and soldiers are often honored by statues paid for by their governments.

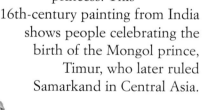

◄ HONORED IN OLD AGE

In many traditional cultures, old people are honored for the wisdom and experience they have gained during their lives. Younger people value what older men and women can teach them. In Asia, Confucius taught that it was a religious duty to respect old people while they were alive, and to make offerings to the spirits of dead ancestors. Very old people, like this dignified man, are regarded as "national treasures" there.

◤ SOLEMN FUNERAL

Priests, a choir, and members of a church congregation escort the coffin containing a dead friend to the graveside in this Polish funeral, held according to the traditions of the Roman Catholic Church. Many religious faiths teach that once a body has been laid to rest, the person's soul or spirit is freed to join God in Heaven or to be punished in Hell.

BIRTHDAYS

Birthdays are celebrated with parties and present-giving—a European and American cultural tradition. Cards are sent, too, and the birthday person is given a cake, decorated with lighted candles. Party guests usually sing the popular song "Happy Birthday to You" (1935).

▶ GETTING MARRIED

A Jewish bride and groom sip wine from a glass during their wedding ceremony as a symbol of the joys and sorrows they will share together in the years ahead. In many cultures, marriage traditionally was considered to be a lifetime's commitment to one person. Most religions still teach this. But in many parts of Europe and the United States today, the tradition has changed—more than half of all marriages end in divorce.

Families

CHILDREN learn a great deal about the values and customs of their culture from other members of their families—particularly grandparents, who are often eager to pass on cultural traditions. Many civilizations place a high value on family life, seeing families as the best place to bring up children or to care for older people. Different cultures have their own ideas about the ideal size and structure of families. One kind is the "nuclear" family —two parents and one or two children. Another kind is the "extended" family, with several generations all living together.

◿ VICTORIAN VALUES

During the reign of Britain's Queen Victoria (1836–1901), families across Europe shared similar social ideals. It was a man's duty to work and provide for his family, while the woman cared for her husband, children, and home.

◱ WORKING TOGETHER

During the 19th century, many families trekked westward across the United States and settled on the harsh prairies of the Midwest. They often lived a long way from their nearest neighbors, and had to be self-reliant and tough to survive. Men, women, and children all had their own "chores," or tasks, to perform on the farm.

◲ UNREAL IDEAL?

In the United States during the 1950s, politicians and preachers urged all women to marry, have children, and stay at home—even though many girls were well educated and wanted to have independent careers. The ideal of the happy family was promoted with pictures like this one, showing a clean, neat, well-dressed family with bright smiles.

◨ MANY GENERATIONS

Today, many families in Europe and North America consist of just two generations—parents and children. But traditionally, families were much larger, as they still are in many other parts of the world. This family from the island of Malta in the Mediterranean extends to four generations—grandparents to great-grandchildren. Often, aunts, uncles, and cousins also share a family home.

◧ DESERT CLAN

For centuries, many families have relied on networks of close relatives, called "clans" or "tribes," to help them survive in harsh places such as the desert. Clan members, like these Bedouins from the deserts of Syria, owe loyalty to a chief and have a duty to help anyone belonging to the same tribe.

ONE CHILD ONLY

To prevent China from becoming overpopulated, the government passed a law forbidding parents to have more than one child. The law slowed the population growth, but sometimes led to problems with over-anxious parents and lonely children.

◨ WORKING MOTHER

In many countries, single mothers are the head of the family. Some are widows and some have never married, but most are divorced. Many mothers—both single and married—work to support their children, and also find time to manage their homes. In some countries, companies provide childcare centers at the office.

Seasons of the year

IN THE past, the seasons played an important part in almost everyone's life. People depended on seasonal rains to water the crops —and if the rains failed, many died. Farmers prepared for the next season in advance, making sure they had the right seeds and tools ready for use. Religious leaders performed rituals asking their gods to send good weather at the most helpful times. And communities joined together to celebrate seasonal festivals such as May Day, Midwinter and harvest time. Today, people are protected from natural hazards by modern buildings, technology, and medicines.

◨ MIDSUMMER GODDESS

Aine, the Irish goddess of love and fertility, was worshiped at Midsummer, when people lit bonfires on her hill. She was believed to be able to command the crops and animals.

◁ NEW YEAR FIREWORKS

In China, New Year is traditionally celebrated by setting off fireworks and firecrackers. The loud bangs are believed to frighten away evil spirits. Families decorate their doorways with streamers of red paper decorated with handwritten poems to bring good luck. Dancers carry huge paper lions and dragons, supported on sticks, through the streets. Clashing cymbals accompany the dancers. And to show their respect, children visit their teachers.

◁ SANTA CLAUS

In many parts of Europe and North America, young children believe that Santa Claus will bring them presents on Christmas Eve. "Santa Claus" is a nickname for St. Nicholas, originally a bishop in Turkey. It was claimed he miraculously restored three young boys to life.

◧ RAIN DANCE

The weather is frequently unpredictable. For thousands of years, people have tried to influence local weather patterns by offering sacrifices to weather gods, saying prayers, or performing rituals. This Japanese rain dancer is wearing a broad-brimmed hat trimmed with a rainlike fringe. The dancer makes rapid movements and chants "magic" words to encourage rain to fall.

SPRING BLOSSOMS

In Japan, families make special trips to the countryside to admire the first cherry blossoms of the year. Spring blooms have inspired many paintings and poems.

◧ FARMING YEAR

Until about 1800, most people lived in the country and relied on the crops they grew and the animals they raised for their survival. The seasons were of far greater significance to most people. Medieval manuscripts, like this one, show peasants performing a "labor" or task for each month of the year. Here, the picture for April shows someone picking fruit in a rainshower, June shows a man plowing, in August the crops are being cut, and in December a pig is about to be killed for a winter feast.

◧ THANKSGIVING

Every year, on the fourth Thursday in November, American families celebrate Thanksgiving Day with a splendid meal. The first Thanksgiving was held in 1621 by settlers in Plymouth Colony, Massachusetts. They wanted to thank God for keeping them safe during the previous year and for sending them a good harvest.

HISTORY OF CULTURE

Celebrations

A CELEBRATION is a time when people get together to express joy at hearing some good news. People often celebrate an individual's achievement, such as exam success or the birth of a new baby. Some celebrations involve larger groups, or even whole nations. A political triumph, such as an election victory, may cause a whole country to cheer, while a religious festival such as Easter may be celebrated in towns and villages across the world. Many celebrations involve eating, giving presents, and wearing special clothes. The normal rules of good behavior are often relaxed as everyone shares in "the festive spirit."

◢ IMPERIAL CORONATION

From 1800 to 1812, Napoleon Bonaparte of France was the greatest general and most powerful ruler in Europe. He celebrated his success by holding a magnificent coronation ceremony for himself and his wife Josephine.

◳ EID UL-FITR

Muslims meet to pray at a mosque in Karachi, Pakistan, during the festival of Eid ul-Fitr—the Festival of Rejoicing. After prayers, many families hold parties for their friends and relatives, and make special gifts to charity. Eid ul-Fitr celebrates the end of the Islamic holy month of Ramadan, when Muslims fast from dawn to dusk to show devotion to Allah (God).

◪ THE END OF PROHIBITION

Between 1919 and 1933, the U.S. government banned the manufacture and sale of all alcoholic drinks. It hoped to end drunkenness and improve public health. When Prohibition finally ended, huge parties were held to celebrate the news.

GRADUATION

Students who have successfully completed his or her studies at college take part in special graduation ceremonies. Each student is given a scroll listing their name and degree.

◢ TRIUMPHAL ARCH

The greatest reward that the Romans could give to an army general was a "triumph"— a public celebration of his military victories. The general's procession marched through the streets and under a triumphal arch.

◣ DIWALI

Hindus and Sikhs celebrate Diwali— a festival of light—in October or November each year. Hindus say prayers to Lakshmi, the goddess of wealth. They decorate their homes with symbols of good fortune and light it with many candles.

◣ CARNIVAL

At carnivals, people dress in magnificent costumes and parade through the streets singing and dancing. This dancer is at the world-famous Rio Carnival in Brazil. Originally, Carnival was a Christian festival held at the beginning of Lent, a period of fasting in February or March—the word "carnival" means "farewell to meat." People held special meals so that they could eat up all the meat that was forbidden in Lent.

Music and dance

BEFORE early humans learned to use language, almost a million years ago, they used body movements and made grunts and squeals to communicate with each other. They also made music by tapping on shells, bones, and wood, and by whistling. Today, simple sounds and body language still play an important part in music and dance. But over thousands of years, the world's many different cultures have developed their own styles of sound and movement to express their feelings. Many are recognizable, and enjoyed by people all over the world.

◀ DOUBLE FLUTE

This Etruscan wall painting, made about 2,500 years ago, shows a young man playing a double flute. The Etruscans lived in central Italy. Like other ancient Mediterranean peoples, they used music in religious ceremonies, as well as for entertainment.

◀ COSSACK DANCER

A Cossack dancer from Ukraine leaps high in the air, showing off his agility. Cossacks were famous for their bravery and horseriding skills, and the men traditionally expressed their warlike energy in dramatic dances.

◀ COUNTRY DANCE

In many parts of northern Europe, people often enjoyed country dancing as a form of entertainment, particularly on long winter evenings. Dressed in traditional costume, this 19th-century Norwegian couple is dancing to the accompaniment of a fiddle, or violin. Traditional country dances feature elaborate patterns of steps. A popular dance for a larger group, or set, is the "square dance," in which four couples face inward from four sides.

◻ CHOIR OF NUNS

From about AD 500 to 1500, the most advanced—and probably the most beautiful—music in Europe was created for choirs of monks or nuns in church. They spent several hours each day chanting prayers and singing hymns. Because they were among the few people who could read and write, their music was written down in books. Many of these have survived, so ancient religious music can still be performed today.

FANCY FOOTWORK

During the 1920s, a new dance called the Charleston caused a sensation. Invented by African-Americans in Charleston, South Carolina, and danced to a jazzy rhythm, it featured fast, high-kicking, backward steps that made women's skirts fly high above the knees!

◿ MUSIC FOR REBELS

Girl members of a Japanese punk rock band strike a defiant pose. For centuries, music has been a popular way of expressing protest against government power or social conventions—unwritten rules of good behavior. Punk rock music originated in England in the 1970s, and was pioneered by bands such as the Sex Pistols. It was raw, energetic, violent, and rebellious.

◻ TEMPLE DANCER

Bharata-natyam is a dance tradition of the Tamil people of southern India. Almost 2,000 years old, it originated among young women who served the gods and goddesses in temples. Seven dances are performed, beginning with a prayer and ending with a reading of ancient holy texts. A singer, drums, and wind instruments accompany the dancer.

Performance

DRAMA—the portrayal on stage of human feelings and relationships—probably developed as a way of acting out myths and legends. Actors were able to bring the stories alive, conveying to an audience a range of emotions—anger, revenge, sorrow, love, and happiness —which the audience could relate to their own lives. The ancient Greeks were the first people to build theaters. Their earliest plays were written for religious festivals —authors competed to have their tragedies or comedies performed. Gradually, over the centuries, different cultures around the world developed their own distinctive forms of drama.

◪ COMIC ACTOR

Roman comic actors, like the one depicted in this terra-cotta model, wore a slave's short tunic and a face mask with a menacing grin. Actors in large Greek and Roman theaters always wore masks, so that people in the back rows of seats could see their expressions. Different masks portrayed different characters— happy, fierce, or sad.

◪ SHAKESPEARE'S GLOBE

William Shakespeare (1564–1616) is considered by most people to have written the greatest plays in the world. Many of them were written to be performed in the circular Globe playhouse in London. Men played all the parts, performing to a noisy audience of nobility and royalty, who sat in wooden bays, and servants, apprentices, and other townsfolk, who stood in front of the central stage.

◪ BEIJING OPERA

During the 18th and 19th centuries, lively, colorful operas were the most popular form of entertainment in China. They were often based on traditional stories or historical events, and featured acrobatic dancing, mock battles, and comedy, as well as singing and orchestral music.

▶ EXPERIMENTAL STYLE

During the 20th century, theater directors in many parts of Europe and the United States experimented with new styles of staging plays. They borrowed ideas from traditional theater in many parts of the world, especially ancient Greece and Japan, and used abstract scenery and dramatic lighting to create powerful moods. Playwrights such as Harold Pinter (b.1930) re-created shocking or depressing scenes from modern life on stage, as in this scene from his play *The Birthday Party*.

☑ RUSSIAN FIRE-EATER

A performer breathes out clouds of fire in a dramatic display of skill in a Russian circus ring. Circuses are over 2,000 years old. They began in ancient Roman times, with horrific gladiator fights, and continued in a smaller way, with animals, jugglers, and acrobats, until around AD 1800. In the 19th century, Philip Astley in Britain and Barnum and Bailey in America re-created spectacular shows to entertain people. Modern circuses often feature high-tech effects, as well as traditional skills.

HARLEQUIN

Masked and dressed in a colorful diamond-patterned costume, Harlequin was the magical character in 18th and 19th century European fairground plays known as "Harlequinades."

☑ MARIE LLOYD, MUSIC HALL STAR

Famous for her cheerful, witty, and sometimes suggestive songs, Marie Lloyd (1870–1922) was the most famous star to entertain audiences in English music halls.

During the late 19th and early 20th centuries, music halls staged twice-nightly shows of about twenty different "turns" or acts. These might include singing, dancing, conjuring, reciting monologues, or telling jokes.
Unusually for that time, many top performers were women, who earned high wages and had many fans.

Films and sound

MOST ideas about culture and civilization are passed from one generation to the next in words, music and visual images. These may be spoken, written, or illustrated in books, or recorded and broadcast by modern media. Over the last two hundred years, new forms of communication have spread cultural ideas worldwide. Before 1900, new printing methods made magazines and newspapers cheap enough for ordinary people to buy. By the 1920s, radio, gramophones, movies, and recorded music provided entertainment for millions of people. After 1950, television became widespread, and today, the Internet brings new words and images to most parts of the world.

◤ **MUTOSCOPE**
Before the invention of films, people could watch moving pictures in a mutoscope. A sequence of images—each slightly different from the last—was mounted on cards inside a drum. When the viewer turned the handle, the images flicked over in rapid succession, giving the illusion of movement. Mutoscopes were a popular form of entertainment in amusement arcades in about 1899. The most popular "show" was called "What the Butler Saw."

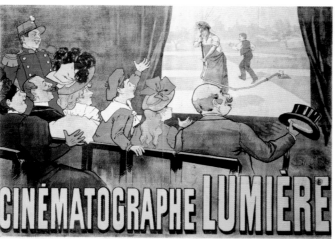

CINÉMATOGRAPHE LUMIÈRE

◤ **MOVIE PIONEERS POSTER**
This colorful poster is advertising the work of the French brothers Auguste and Louis Lumière, two of the world's most important cinema pioneers. In 1895, they invented the Cinématographe—a machine that combined a movie camera and film projector in one.

◗ **GRAMOPHONE**
The first-ever recorded sentence was "Mary had a little lamb." It was cut into a tinfoil cylinder and played on a phonograph, invented by Thomas Edison in 1877. Soon, record designers were able to improve the accuracy of recordings. By 1894, German-born Emile Berliner had designed the gramophone, a machine that played disk-shaped records of sung or spoken words. It amplified the sound through a bell-shaped horn.

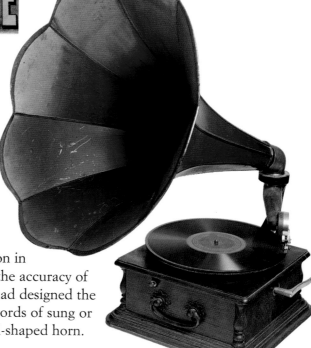

◨ SILENT-MOVIE CAMERA

The first movies were silent. Large cameras were used to film the actors, who spoke their lines as if in a normal performance. On screen, their lip movements could be seen, but no spoken sounds were heard by the audience. In the cinema, a pianist or organist played live music to create the right mood for each scene. The first "talkies," in which spoken words were heard, were made in the 1920s.

◨ MOVIE-STAR GLAMOR

After about 1920, film stars, such as Oscar-winning actress Audrey Hepburn (1929–93), attracted huge numbers of admirers. Although very well paid, movie stars had little privacy, and their lives were controlled by the movie makers.

◨ THE MUSIC INDUSTRY

Whitney Houston performs live at a Nelson Mandela benefit concert. Since beginning her singing career at the age of 11 in a gospel choir, Whitney has gone on to sell 75 million records in the United States alone, through Arista Records. The music industry developed rapidly during the 1950s, when the first long-playing vinyl records and hi-fi (high fidelity) gramophones were developed. About the same time, popular music shows were broadcast on TV, creating a vast audience for the latest sounds.

MICROPHONES

First invented in 1878, microphones are devices that convert sound energy into electrical energy. Modern microphones are small and lightweight, and are linked to amplifiers to increase the volume of sound in live performances.

Global village

DURING the 1960s, Canadian cultural historian Marshall McLuhan (1911–80) suggested that 20th-century electronic communications had turned the world into a "global village." He described how large amounts of information, flowing from one country to another, were destroying cultures. He also predicted that the ideas, beliefs, and values of wealthy superpowers, like the United States, would overwhelm traditional lifestyles. By the year 2000, many people thought his predictions had come true.

◪ TEA PICKING IN JAPAN

Drinking tea is a strong cultural tradition in many parts of the world—notably Japan, China, India, and Britain. In much of Asia, the people who grow and pick the tea are poor workers, while those who enjoy it are rich consumers. Since the 1980s, fair-trade organizations have campaigned to improve working conditions for producers and to increase their pay.

◪ SOCCER

All over the world, children love playing and watching soccer. One of the favorite teams, as far apart as India and Africa, is Britain's Manchester United! Together, sport and global communications have successfully united people from widely different cultures.

◪ FINANCIAL POWER

Billions of dollars change hands every day as brokers do deals in the world's financial markets, such as the Tokyo Stock Exchange. As they buy and sell shares in companies, dealers influence the financial future of countless people in foreign countries, raising or lowering food and fuel prices.

BACKPACKERS

Undeveloped countries are popular vacation destinations for backpackers from wealthy nations. Travel provides an exciting adventure and a chance to see and learn about other people's cultures firsthand. But the influence of foreign travelers' customs can undermine local traditions.

◪ THE POWER OF RADIO

Cheap transistor radios have revolutionized communications in many inaccessible regions, where there are no regular newspapers, and where hardly anyone can read. The radio brings the latest news from all over the world, as well as all kinds of entertainment, from dramas to soap operas.

◪ MULTINATIONAL BRANDS

Multinational corporations that produce popular brands of food and drink are always eager to find new buyers for their goods. Often, the goods become status symbols for consumers in poorer countries, who choose them in preference to cheaper local brands. Some economists argue that the multinational brands harm the local economies by transferring money from poor countries to rich ones.

◪ INTERNET CAFÉ

The Internet began in 1969, when it was funded by the U.S. Department of Defense. Military planners used the international computer network (the World Wide Web) to gather information. Today, the Internet is massive and constantly being updated. No single organization can control it. Users anywhere in the world who have access to a computer and telephone line—often through Internet cafés like this one in Singapore—can search for information.

Glossary

ADORNMENTS
Accessories, usually added to something to make it look more attractive. People also wear adornments such as jewelry, or hair accessories, such as plaits or bows.

ANCESTORS
People who lived in the past, and from whom other people are directly descended. For example, a child's direct ancestors are its parents, then grandparents, great grandparents, and so on.

ANECDOTE
A short and often humorous narrative of an incident, usually involving real-life situations.

BACKPACKER
A person who goes hiking, usually with just a rucksack to hold supplies. Backpackers very often travel throughout entire countries like this, with minimal supplies.

BARBECUE
When food is grilled outside over an open grill or fire, or the name given to an outside party where this happens.

BEDOUINS
Members of an Arab tribe who are nomadic (move from place to place to live). Bedouins live in large tents in the deserts of the Middle East. They move from place to place with their livestock, looking for suitable places to camp.

CAREER
The job, occupation, or profession of a particular person, such as nurse, or teacher. A career often provides good opportunities for advancement and promotion.

CEREMONY
A formal act, convention, or event carried out according to custom or traditional rules, usually performed to honor and continue some kind of past ritual, rite, or anniversary.

CHRONICLE
A continuous record of historical events, written in the order of time that they occurred, usually year by year.

CIVILIZATION
A people, their society and culture which have developed in a social, political, and technological sense, and are refined in interests and tastes.

CLAN
A group of people, usually from the same family and sharing the same surname, led by one chief, and who have a common ancestor. Or, a group of people who have similar interests or concerns.

CONFUCIUS (551–479 BC)
The first great Chinese philosopher. The name means "king without a crown." His discussions are collected in *The Analects.*

CORONATION
The ceremony that involves the crowning of a king or queen.

CORPORATION
A business, or a body of people, that are authorized by law to act jointly as an individual, for example the council of a city, or a company.

COSSACK
A member of a free peasant people in Southeast Russia, a cavalry man, also known for a certain style of dancing.

CUSTOM
A traditional practice, usually established by a particular community of people.

EPIC
A very long story, poem, or tale, told in an elevated style, which relates many great and magnificent deeds, especially involving a hero or heroine.

ETHNIC
Something that relates to a group of people of the same race and cultural tradition, such as dress, food, or customs.

FAMINE
A severe shortage of food that is the result of poor weather, leading to crop failure. Famine can also be caused by an increase in population. It generally results in a high death toll.

FLAPPER
A young, fashionable woman of the 1920s, who wore frivolous clothes and sported short hair, and who often displayed unconventional behavior.

GENERATION
Relating to people of the same age and period in time. This also applies to the single stage of natural descent of people or a family. This is usually about 30–33 years.

GLOBAL
Affecting or relating to the entire world, or taking into consideration all the peoples of the world.

GRADUATION
The receiving of a higher-education degree or a high school diploma. The term is often used to describe the ceremony denoting this act.

HARLEQUIN
A character from traditional Italian plays who wore a black mask and a brightly colored diamond patterned costume.

HIGH FIDELITY
An accurate and high-quality reproduction of sound, so much so that it seems indistinguishable from the original.

INDUSTRIAL REVOLUTION
The last quarter of the 18th-century in Britain that saw the rapid development of industries such as cotton and wool. This led to increased mechanization and mass production in factories.

INITIATION
The acceptance of someone into a group or society, for example, after he or she has taken part in an introductory ceremony.

MASS MEDIA
The way in which information and news are communicated to the general public, usually by way of television, radio, and the press.

MAY DAY
The first day of May. It is often celebrated as a spring festival and marks the revival of life after the cold of winter.

MEDIEVAL
Usually referring to the Middle or Dark Ages, a 1,000-year period in history, which generally began at the end of the Roman era, around 400 AD, and ended with the Renaissance period, around 1400 AD.

MIDSUMMER
The period of time in the middle of summer around the solstice—June 21 in the Northern Hemisphere or December 21 in the Southern Hemisphere. This day is the longest of the year in terms of hours of daylight.

MINSTREL
An entertainer of historical times who usually sang and played musical instruments; some minstrels were given permanent positions or jobs in the households of the rich.

MUSIC HALL
Usually a type of theater or concert hall, in which musical entertainment can be seen.

NOBILITY
People of aristocratic birth, or of a higher rank. This also relates to people with greatness of mind or character.

NOMADIC
The way in which people wander from place to place in search of food and shelter, making makeshift homes as they go. These people do not settle in one place for very long.

OPERA
A dramatic play in which the words are sung, accompanied by an orchestra. The play usually tells a story of great tragedy or love.

PILGRIMAGE
A journey to a shrine or other holy place, undertaken to gain a sense of closeness to a religion or to reaffirm one's faith.

PROHIBITION
The complete ban on the manufacture and sale of alcohol in the U.S. from 1920–1933.

PROJECTOR
A machine, such as a movie projector, that casts an enlarged image, either still or moving, onto a screen, wall, or some other smooth surface.

REBELS
People who resent and who fight against oppressive conditions or governments, or refuse to conform to authority.

RITUAL
A ceremony or event that is always carried out in the same way, according to strict rules, often for religious purposes.

SACRIFICE
Giving something precious to a king, god, or deity, such as a treasured possession, food, the life of an animal or a person, often in exchange for a need, such as to stop something bad.

SCRIPTURES
The religious writings of a particular religion. For example, the scriptures of the Christian religion are found in the Bible.

SEGREGATION
The separating of groups, usually to isolate a racial or ethnic minority from the rest of society.

STATUS SYMBOL
Something that denotes wealth, or a higher social standing, usually a possession, such as a car, or a house.

STOCK EXCHANGE
The market where the trading of stocks and shares is carried out by professional dealers.

SUPERMARKET
A self-service store, where people can buy food and household goods. Supermarkets were first established in the U.S. in the 1930s. Originally they sold only food. Some modern supermarkets are huge, selling a wide range of goods.

TREK
To make a long and difficult journey, such as those carried out by families in the early 19th century, hoping to settle on the prairies of the U.S.

YURT
A large tent made of animal skins, used as shelter by nomadic (wandering) peoples on the Russian Steppes.

Index

ACKNOWLEDGMENTS

Art Archive: Page 12 (t/l) British Library, (t/r) Archaeological Museum Lima/Dagli Orti, (c) Eileen Tweedy, 13 (t/l) Real biblioteca de lo Escorial/Dagli Orti, (t/r) Private Collection Paris/Dagli Orti, 14 (c) Victoria and Albert Museum London/Eileen Tweedy, 15 (b) Chester Brummel, 18 (t/r) Musée des Arts Décoratifs Paris/Dagli Orti, 20 (c) British Library/Eileen Tweedy, 24 (c/l) Art Archive, 25 (c/l) Osterreichisches National Bibliothek Vienna/Harper Collins Publishers, 26 (t/r) Musée du Château de Versailles/Dagli Orti, (b/r) Dagli Orti, 27 (t/r) Album/Joseph Martin, 28 (t/r) Dagli Orti, (b/l) Edward Grieg House, Nordas Lake/Dagli Orti, 29 (t/l) British Library, 30 (t/l) British Museum/Eileen Tweedy, 31 (c/l) Museum der Stadt Wien/Dagli Orti, 32 (c/l) Musée de l'Affiche Paris/Dagli Orti, 33 (t/r) Art Archive **Corbis:** Page 8 (c/l) David & Peter Turnley, 9 (t/l) Staffan Widstrand, (b/l) Hulton-Deutsch Collection, 16 (t/r) Michael S. Yamashita, 17 (b) Macduff Everton, 21 (c/l) David & Peter Tumley, 23 (t/r) Bob Krist, (c/l) Dave Bartruff, 25 (b) Steve Chenn, 27 (c/l) Stephanie Maze, (b) Stephanie Maze, 29 (c) Catherine Kamow, 30 (b) Michael S. Yamashita, 31 (t/r) Hulton-Deutsch Collection, (b) Jeffrey L.Rotman, 33 (b/r) Corbis, 34 (c) David & Peter Tumley, 35 (t/l) Danny Lehman, (b) Macduff Everton **Kobal:** Page 8 (b) Disney, 13 (c/l) MGM, (b/r) Lucas Film/20th Century Fox, 32 (t/r) Kobal Collection, 33 (c/l) Paramount

All other photographs are from:
MKP Archives; Corel Corporation; Photodisk